We Go on a
Train

by Joanne Mattern

Red Chair Press   Egremont, Massachusetts

Look! Books are produced and published by Red Chair Press:

Red Chair Press LLC   PO Box 333   South Egremont, MA 01258-0333

www.redchairpress.com

 FREE Educator Guides at www.redchairpress.com/free-resources

Publisher's Cataloging-in-Publication Data
Names: Mattern, Joanne, 1963–
Title: We go on a train / by Joanne Mattern.
Other Titles: Train

Description: Egremont, Massachusetts : Red Chair Press, [2019] | Series:
    Look! books. Ways we go | Includes glossary and "Good to Know" fact
    boxes. | Interest age level: 004-007. | Includes bibliographical
    references and index. | Summary: "What to expect from a trip on a
    train."--Provided by publisher.

Identifiers: ISBN 9781634406307 (library hardcover) | ISBN 9781634406420
    (paperback) | ISBN 9781634406369 (ebook) | LCCN 2018955662

Subjects: LCSH: Transportation--Juvenile literature. | Railroad trains--
    Juvenile literature. | CYAC: Transportation. | Railroad trains.

Classification: LCC HE152 .M386 2019 (print) | LCC HE152 (ebook) | DDC 388
    [E]--dc23

Photo credits: All iStock except for the following: pp. 8, 14, 18, 19
Shutterstock; pp. 17 Alamy.

Printed in United States of America

0519 1P CGF19

Table of Contents

A First Train Ride

Have you ever ridden on a train? People ride trains every day. Some train rides are short. Other train rides are long. Some trains travel thousands of miles!

At the Station

A train ride starts at the train **station**. **Passengers** buy tickets. You can buy your ticket from a machine. Or you can buy your ticket at the window.

People wait for the train on the **platform**. Some train stations are small. Others are very big. These have many different platforms.

All Aboard!

Here comes the train! The train whistle blows loud and long. Stay behind the line until the train stops and the doors open. Then you can **board** the train.

Good to Know

The first trains were powered by steam. Steam built pressure that caused the train to move as it released, like a whistle in a teakettle.

Look for a seat on the train. The **conductor** comes through to take everyone's tickets. He or she might punch your ticket to show where you got on the train.

Riding the Train

The train rides along. It passes buildings and trees. The train stops at each station. People get off. People get on.

Good to Know

The longest train trip in the world runs across Russia into China.

A Long Trip

Most trains have rows of seats. Long-distance trains also have private rooms. You can sleep in tiny bunk beds. That looks like fun!

Long-distance trains have special cars. The lounge car has big windows. You can watch the **scenery** go by. The dining car is where you go for meals.

Some trains have special cars like a small cafe.

19

Last Stop

The train pulls into the station. Get up and grab your things. Step off onto the train platform. Did you like your first train ride?

Words to Know

board: to get on a vehicle

conductor: a person in charge of a vehicle who collects tickets

passengers: people who travel in a vehicle

platform: a flat area where people wait for a train

scenery: natural things and places, such as trees or mountains

station: a stopping place for a train, subway, or bus

Learn More at the Library

Books (Check out these books to learn more.)

Leighton, Christina. *Passenger Trains.* Bellwether Media, 2018.

Kenan, Tessa. *Trains.* Tadpole Books, 2019.

Spaight, Anne J. *Trains on the Go.* Lerner Publications, 2016.

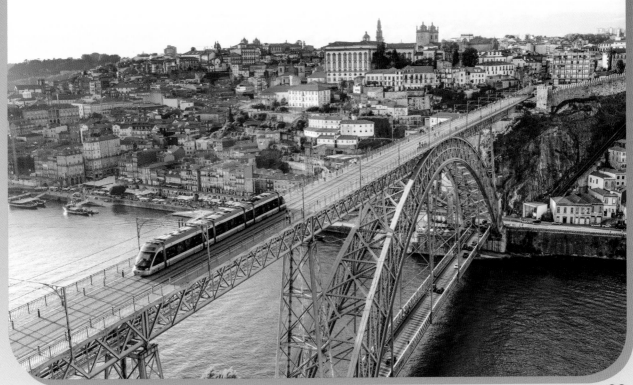

Index

About the Author

Joanne Mattern has written hundreds of nonfiction books for children. She likes writing about different people and places. Joanne lives in New York State with her family.